A Bro
Never Broken

**Written by
Tiara J Church
Illustrated By
Ivan Sivek
Dominique Wilkins**

Copyright © 2012 Tiara J Church, All Rights Reserved.
For permission to use or reproduce contents of this book email churchpublished@gmail.com
Manufactured and Published in the U.S.A

Sometimes people in a relationship go through ups and downs. Sometimes we never really learn from our mistakes. So I dedicate this book to all that ever been through the ups and downs of a relationship and still didn't quite get the hang of it yet. Those that walk around with their heads down and their hearts empty. I want you to know that no matter how much you cry, how hard it gets your heart will fix if you let it. You will never forget that love you had, just remember the fact that they lost the best thing that happened to them. You can't love someone else unless you truly are happy with yourself. So find yourself and the right one will find you. As long as you have control over your feelings, A Broken Heart is Never Broken. Remember that there is someone for everyone; you just have to be patient.

Dedicated to;

I would like to dedicate this book to the women I've met, I haven't met, and who I've yet to meet. I would like to dedicate this story to all the survivors and the ones who left behind a legacy of lessons learned. I would like to send a special dedication out to our young ladies, whose eyes need to be opened and made aware of the possibility, that this could be your situation. To all of my young men, I would like to make aware that this is not okay. At times we overlook and brush off things until they hit home, consider this a dry run. Many would never admit it, but this is also dedicated to the men out there. The ones that saw firsthand from their mother or other loved ones. The ones that have experienced it themselves and most of all the ones with daughters who will need to know how to handle/understand it. It starts at home let it end there break the chain, each one teach one, let's get through this together. I love you, you deserve better.

Table of Contents

Love Begins....
1. If I didn't have you
2. The Message
3. I Think I Found the One
4. Soul mates
5. Out of all the Reasons
6. Love or Lust
7. There's More
8. Untitled
9. Just Walk Away
10. For What it's Worth
11. Temptation or Fate
12. Is my Heart Enough?
13. Remember our Past!
14. Chances are....
15. What is it?
16. Change of Heart
17. Misunderstood
18. Selfish Love
19. L.I.K.E
20. What do we Gain?

Signs of Change....
21. INTRO
22. I Never Thought
23. Switch
24. The Time has come
25. One more Try
26. Little things
27. Love (As a Person)
28. Like Father, Like Son
29. My Lover, My Friend

30. Reasons
Points of No Return…
31. Quiet Before the Storm
32. Drunken Love
33. Battered
34. 9 months
35. Call for help
36. Guilty as Charged
37. 2 Sided
38. Cycle
39. Mistakenly Done
40. Should've, Could've, Would've
41. The unseen scars (of a battered woman)
42. Double victim
43. Overflow
44. Lesson Learned
45. Us
46. End of Line
47. Done
Reconstruction…
48. Intro (I Use to Love)
49. After the Storm
50. Love?
51. Questions
52. The Line is So Thin
53. Woman Scorned
54. A Tale of Two hearts
55. Good-bye Past
56. Love Yourself
57. Suicide
58. A Broken Heart is Never Broken
59. Thanked and Forgiven
60. Reconstruction (complete)

Love Begins....

If I Didn't Have You

The world wouldn't be enough if in fact you were gone.
Not only would it be nothing, I would be all alone.
I'd miss you too much and the rivers would run dry.
I'd remember your warm smile and the sun would fall from the sky.
Oh what would encourage you to leave me so blue?
After all you said and the things we went through.
But that's only an assumption I know you love your girl.
You couldn't leave me here because I live in your world.
So sleep on my darling and dream of far away.
And when you awaken sweet whispers you would say:

"As long as we live in harmony, we should never divide from 1 to 2.
Because my lover my friend, love is our glue.
But if ever it shall happen that from earth you disappear.
Never do you have to worry your heart will keep us near.
Only thing that can separate us is if our love glue should begin to wear.
But never my darling should I stop and not care.

My world would be nothing, if in fact you are gone.
Not only would it be nothing I would be all alone.
I'd miss you so much that the rivers would run dry.
I'd remember your warm smile then the sun would fall from the sky.
So that will never happen and our love shall never wear.
I will tell you "I love you" and our world we will always share".

The Message

Don't tell me things you don't really mean.
Don't lead me to believe what you're telling me.
You just don't think after you've done wrong.
These problems are yours too; you can't just
"Move On."
I listen to you because you always had the
right things to say.
I just don't know why you act this way.
I feel confused and weak in the knee.
I feel that no matter what I do, you'll never
understand me.
I think about you day in and day out.
But how often do you think about me?
It kills me inside that I want to call.
It hurts me that I want you that's all.
How do I fight my very long and old ways?
To be selfish and kind the mixture never pays.
I want to share with you my eternity.
That's how I feel when you're next to me.
You take my breath away, without you I can't
breathe.
I can't sit here without you on my mind.
I try to drown out the thoughts, by writing or
singing a song.
I know this is a long message but I never felt
this way about someone for this long.

Beeeeeep.

I Think I Found the One

How do you know if the one you found is the one that's right?
How do you know if the one you found is worth the fight?
When do you realize love is what you got?
When you realize you want that one a lot.
What move do you make or do you let them take the lead?
What steps do you take to plant the seed!
Who would have known a life that one would start with me!
Who could I tell that we will always be?
Where do I start to describe my good find?
Where do I go if our love is in my mind?
Why do I need to realize that it's real?
Why do I need to wonder, because I know how I feel?

Soul Mates

You're the one I been searching for high and low.
You're the one that my heart beats for.
I now understand love to its fullest extent.
Together forever you and I were meant.
I never felt this sensation before in my heart.
Even when I'm mad at you or we are apart.
I still don't care who was wrong or right.
I just want us to make up from our fight.
My love for you is real, so pure, so true.
I couldn't have had a better soulmate than you.
You're the sunshine after my stormy day.
You're the hand I use to wipe my tears away.
You're that constant reminder in my heart.
That keeps me from just falling apart.
You're the smile that always pushes away my frown.
You're the only one fit to wear my crown.
I miss you more than I miss my childhood years.
I'm so secure with you that I forget about my fears.
I realize now that no other soul could compare.
I couldn't see love until you answered my prayers.
I'm so glad I found you I love you so much!

Out of All the Reasons

Out of all the happiness I have ever found

I believe the one I share with you make me proud

I hope this good I have last for awhile

Cause everyday with you brings a smile

I don't need to pretend for you

For once someone sees me and loves me too

From all the past lies, pain, and deceit

I feel better you now, make me complete

Out of all the reasons I think to be

I'm glad that you are with me.

Love or Lust

Deep in my heart I feel it begin to rust.
Something's telling me this feeling I feel I shouldn't trust.
No life to live with you this is a cover.
No way possible for you to be my lover.
How can I doubt this, when for this I've worked?
I feel no love just as my heart's been jerked.
How or why did this happen to me?
But I know the answer, since I see what I want to see.
From the start you said it, did I hear, not at all.
I just heard bells ringing; thought love finally answered my call.
How could I be so stupid, if I'm so smart?
This is a blow that will stick to the heart.
You call, and then hang up, you don't want to talk.
I guess you're saying my life with you just came to a halt
I didn't know the difference between love and lust.
I keep falling for this trick, allowing my body to trust.
Nothing else to say, this didn't come easy.
You don't have to explain just to please me.
My heart is shaking I feel my knees breakdown.
I just hope one day I could figure it out.
I end this conversation with nothing to say.
I just wish I didn't have to feel this way.

There's more....!

There's more to being happy than living with a smile.
Than dreaming far away and going a far mile.
There's more to a relationship then sexual activity.
Than lying in the bed and having your way with me.
I know what I'm saying will catch you off guard.
I rather write it though because saying it is just too hard.
Our relationship is good going the way it should go.
I just wanted to tell you, I just wanted you to know.
That there's more to life than knowing only of your own hurt
Than being by yourself and doing all the work.
There's more to love than your eyes can see.
Than all the sadness and the pain in you and in me.
I wanted to tell you my feelings, my thoughts.

Our lack of communication a problem it has brought.
With it our relationship is stronger and can never be torn
And as long as you know and understand that there's more.

Untitled

I love you, but you're gone away.
I want to talk, but you have nothing to say.
I know you, but do I really know.
I saw you, but where did you go?
Our world is changing, but only I can see.
You are becoming mean, only to me
The way you act, don't hurt you.
The words you say, hurt me too!
We are the same and different at times.
We think on our own and have different state of mind.
We know wrong from right and still say mean things.
We don't need money or a diamond ring.
I just want you to come back.
I just want you to realize it's assurance you lack.
I don't want you to go out of your way.
I just want for you to come home and say...
You know that I'm hurt and say listen boo...
I love you too!

Just Walk Away

Hiding from me are shadows in the night.
Twisting and turning I can't sleep at night.
Everywhere I turn another shadow come to be.
Why do I not see their faces but they see me?
Names that I've heard but I don't recognize them.
Oh my, that name I know him!
I open my eyes to know it's not a dream.
Everything I see and hear is exactly what it seem.
You keep walking past but the shadows hide your face.
As I walk closer you start at a faster pace.
I head home with tears in my eyes that shine so bright.
I just wish you would speak up and step into the light.
I just sit here and worry as seconds, minutes and hours past.
I just wonder how long this strange feeling will last.
You walk away, you ride.
Your lying, secrets you hide.
Secrets that should be shared, like the rest of you.
To my knowledge you never lied until now, you're with who.

I close my eyes to wish all bad far away.
In the darkness I just sit in the silence and pray.
Whatever wrong you have done, you make it right.
I just hope, wish and pray you're finish by tonight.
I've grown suspicious of your actions and lies.
What about our hearts or for that matter mines?
Do you not even wonder how I feel or what I care.
Of course you wouldn't know I'm hurting if you're not there.
Just go home and sleep until the break of day.
Even though you've changed we don't have to be this way.
We can make it better before it gets any worst.
Don't make me believe every good in my life is a curse.
Whatever you have to do, please do it another day.
Tonight baby just for me, walk away.

For What it's Worth

How far do you go how much do you take.
Before you up and leave for
good or just break.
 How long do you bite your tongue for its
worth you don't know.
Since for you, what you look for, it don't
show.
You try and you try to stick in there and
hang on. But for what, if the street was a
two way it wouldn't be wrong. You would be
happy and that's what you should want,
right! Yet you're sticking it out and you're
the only one left to fight. They have given
up at least on your part. So you should to,
because you'll never win their heart. It's
gone. It's taken and you're being pulled
along. That's why it seems as if it's not
getting better, and it seems like it will
always be wrong. You have to endure too
much, you have to suck it all in. And for
what they only love you as a friend. It's not
worth it, not the beginning or the end. You
have to step back to see the picture for
what it is. All that was and will be and of
course all that is. Rules set by someone
else as you play in their court. So when do
you forfeit the game and realize you fell
short? When do you stand up and speak
out to the ref or do you just walk out and

away with what is left. You chose your own way life has a choice for you. Are you gone stick it out and take this sh*# or walk out- What to do?

Temptation or Fate?

How do you tell someone you feel for them?
If all you can say is that you love, HIM.
Are there any other words that can describe the way you feel?
Or do you have to take that and believe that it's real!
Is there such a thing as fake love?
Or is this just a test from above?
Do you believe in love at first sight?
Or is your mind and heart in a fight?
Why do you blindly see what you have?
You know that one that makes you laugh!
Why do you deafly hear what he says to you?
You know when he says he loves you and you love him, too!
How can you be tempted to care for another soul?
When the love you blindly see is all you know!
Does that mean that it's not true!
Is the conclusion's up to you?
Do your answers lie deep in your heart?
And you really knew the answer from the start!
But you close out that assumption and believe what you're told!
So now looking for the answer you put your

life on hold!
Could it be possible this new feeling is fate?
Or is it possible you are confused and it you hate?
Could it be possible that you found in another what you want in your, man?
And because of this a conclusion you can't land?
Is it that your love life is moving into soon?
And the words of another are tempting you.
To think that you have feelings that you think you feel.
But deep down inside, your heart knows it's not real.
Your heart keeps telling you over and over again.
That, that other guy is only your friend.
What you feel is not only what it seem.
It's only a feeling in which you dream!
Whether its fate or temptation that drives you away.
In love with that one you will always stay.
Temptation may lead you and bring another hand.
But fate was the one that made you love that man.
Whether it was forever or just for a day.
Never should temptation lead fate astray!

Is my Heart Enough?

To satisfy your cravings that's extremely strong.
Too want for love and affection for so long.
Now that you have it you're scared of what will happen to you.
Scared of all the things love might put you through.
You try to pretend you don't feel what you feel.
I think you should know that the good beat is real.
The way your eyes close as we kiss.
As if none of this memory you want to miss.
The way your eyes twinkle when you say you love me.
Shows me that you're telling the truth and we'll always be.
Now we've gotten closer you've gotten my all.
Now I feel that there's a shortage in your call.
I still see that twinkle in your eyes but it doesn't feel the same way.
"And that I love you baby," that you lack to say.
You're taking me for granted and don't see how I feel.
I know that your heart has told you our love is real.

What do I need to do to prove to you I care.
What do I need to say to show you I'll always be there?
Nothing I say seems to hit you it can work it's not that tough.
I'll just leave you to think of the situation and ask
"Is my Heart Enough"

Remember our past

Don't you remember when we first got together?
It was a late August day with nice cool weather.
Since then you would meet me and greet me.
With a warm hug and a smile would come to be.
Every day I came home before my door I would stop at yours and say.
I would talk to you love you as we play.
I remember this because then we were so close.
But now were not I don't know what happened though.
One minute we're happy the next I'm guessing.
Now there are no more hugs and kisses when we greet.
Only my heart will remember how we use to meet.
I got use to our old ways now you changed.
I was your friend and your lover I use to be close ranged.
But lately my darling you've kept us apart.
Do I still have a place inside your heart?
It's changing, our love, our life isn't what it seem.
So what will happen to the love in which I dream?

Chances Are....

Chances are you want to go back to you old ways.
Not committed just playing girls and having sex slaves.
Chances are you are just bored with me.
And you are acting it out so well making it hard to see.
You are just leading me on making me think our love is, strong.
When the truth is that it's gone all wrong.
I'm trying my hardest to look at it a little different.
But every time I see you there's another hint.
Chances are you still talk to your old freak.
Keeping her posted on what day of the week.
Chances are that's why I'm drifting from you.
That's why you don't tell me what you do.
You just string me along thinking I don't see the clue.
The secrets and the short conversations with you.
What do you expect from me I know the game.
If it's like that let go playing games are lame.
Chances are that's where you're at when,

you leave here.
That would be smart get a girl that's near.
Chances are she even knows my name.
It could be possible the girls are the same.
I know it's hard to change and commit.
But this is something good keep me out that shit.
I've told you once I'll tell you again.
Just watch your back don't get caught my friend.
Chances are you'll be back.
Chances are you'll see the love they lack.

What Is It?

What's it about love no one understand?
To be there for someone as much as you can.
Be a man to a woman and woman to a man.
To say I love you means just as stated!
But when people use it it's always gold-plated.
There's a different meaning that's related.
To be in a relationship is the start of it all.
It's when every day you wait on a call.
But every day you don't get it, you have to stand tall.
To be committed isn't what it used to be.
What you feel isn't what they see.
Now you change the locks he won't return the key.
What is it about love they just don't get?
To be in a relationship now is not worth shit.

Change of Heart

I can't let you hurt me
So I have to move on.
The things you're doing are
Becoming clearly shown.
You're doing what you said you
would never lead me to believe.
I thought that one day
love we would achieve.
But how can we accomplish
something we don't talk about.
It used to be sweet and to
me I love you, you shout.
Now you don't even talk
to me as much as you should.
Sometimes I feel you wouldn't
even if you could.
I gave you my everything and
you gave me none in return.
But even so, to love with
no strings I had to learn.
The love I had for you
kept building stronger.
But I don't think I can
take it any longer.
I wanted my first love
to last for awhile.
But I guess this is just
another relationship on file.
Don't ever think that you'll forever
have a place in my heart.
Because we either need to change

or just be apart.
You can't blindly keep
loving someone like me.
Because all the good in the
relationship you can't see.
I could never just blame
it all on you.
Because to have a relationship
it takes TWO.
I know your heart is
in the right place.
But maybe your mind
just need some space.
You're not ready to
commit to one girl.
But when you are I'll be there when
the doors open to your world.
So good-bye my old friend
I hope life bring you joy.
If it should ever rain in
your heart my heart is home boy.
I'll take you in and shelter
you from harm.
I know you'll get far though,
because of your charm.
Well I guess I better leave you be.
But one day I hope you'll
find another love like me.

Misunderstood

To "You" someone I thought was different.
I never thought in a trivia I would need a hint.
Everyone has their secrets and everyone has rain.
I just looked past the fact that mines would be your gain.
How could this have happened when did it have to be me.
You said you wouldn't hurt me but that's not what I see.
I look at you and wonder who you are.
Cause the man I see stand before me is from me standing too far.
How could I ever get past the scar that crosses my heart?
Knowing the one who did it will forever my life be apart.
How could you face the mirror or wear a smile each day.
Knowing that the heart I wear is the one that has to pay.
I would like to take a vowel that spells out understand.
Let's go on a little journey if you would please take my HAND....
You say that you are misunderstood and no one ever tries.
How could you truly know that if you love

with closed eyes?
I think that you Then sheltered yourself, and now have lost your way.
Been blinded by the trickery and you don't know with whom to stay.
You hide behind the words "I'm Misunderstood" 'cause you don't know who you are!
So you look for one who's good at puzzles to put the pieces back by far.
No matter though, how far anyone can get. If they are missing the center piece no other ones will fit.
So I ask myself how can one's love be so true.
When "misunderstood" you, you're clueless about you.
You've lost your way and you're seeking "you" once again.
But you shouldn't bring others into it my friend.
This is a self journey for you have to do alone.
If you don't open your eyes soon it will be gone.
Lost forever for not even you will understand.
How you stood in the mirror and saw another Man.
To you I know is someone different from the one I use to know

hurry now and open your eyes for your heart, you have to show.

Selfish Love

Maybe you should just try to change.
It seems as if for your love I'm truly out of range.
Truthfully I don't know why you have to lie.
I thought we were good now we are saying good-bye.
Maybe you should have just told me.
What you wanted me to understand and see.
It seems as if we will grow apart.
Without reason, a try, a brand new start.
I wanted so much to be your one and only.
I just don't know what came over me.
Communication it was not our part.
Doing what you did hurt my feelings, broke my heart.
Maybe it's me blindly showing you what you needed to see.
I've tried so hard to please you.
Since you weren't satisfied, now we're through.

L. I. K. E

Love is hard to overcome
but it's a lot of good in it.

I quit putting my heart on the line because I
had my share of this sh*#.

Kindness comes and goes just like some men.
But what is it about both you get caught up in.

Everyone knows what a hard time
feels like and how it comes to be.
But not everyone gives up LIKE me.

What do We Gain?

Nobody told me it would be this way.
But most dudes leave a girl every day.
I wonder what's the point of a relationship.
When someone else comes along they just dip.
What is the point of waiting for love?
Nothing can help your heart not even up above.
So what made God invent emotions and sh*#.
We could have been like robots and never felt it.
I use to think only I would never fall for anyone.
Now I know for a fact love for me is done.
No more boys to have relations, no more tries.
No more getting caught up in their lies.
Then I remember it's not up to me.
This is the way God wants it to be.
You know he's a guy.
Because only the women cry.
Never can a man walk in a woman's shoes.
Only thing they know is how to give them blues.
You know what I have nothing else to say.
I just wish men could go through it all one day.
Then their butts would know how it feel.
And every word they say is "We think" it's for real.

Signs of Change…

INTRO.....

My love for you is deep, I can't go on.
My feelings are growing weak, I can't make them strong.
I love you I do, but how do I know.
That the love you had for me you didn't let go.
As I open my eyes, I realize what I felt the most.
That to someone else you were playing host.
My life would have once revolved around you.
But now no longer do you call me you're boo.

I Never Thought!!

I never thought I could love so deep.
That I didn't realize what I needed to see.
The once so passionate love, I thought you held for me.
Was simply just a dream, a fantasy?
Let's take a trip to the first time we met.
Don't you remember the childish game?
Of hiding the way we feel, when we feel the same.
I could just picture in the back of my mind.
You was so sweet to me, you was so kind.
We played, kissed and hugged each other.
No thoughts in our head of another.
I remember you use to hold my hand.
Letting everyone know you were my man.
I remember when you put me out.
And never after I exit the last do you shout.
Those were the days I remember them well.
It seems like now all of it is hell.
Let's move on...
I remember when we went on our first date.
When we went to get gyros and we shot pool instead.
It was so romantic we were the only ones there.
Just to be with you, I wouldn't care.
Don't you remember our first Christmas together?

The warmth in our heart could've changed the weather.
I can't forget how you gave me a weekend for my birthday.
And a movie trip I didn't want to end.
Now look we also share a child.
Whose life is so lovely and so mild?
Now we share our first anniversary.
But it seems there will be no more with me.
I Never Thought....
It would have changed like this.
What part of our relationship did I miss?
The fact that now you're better than me.
Is the role of our lives changed for thee?
Do you not see me as you use to.
Now that I'm pregnant, I'm not your boo.
You said you'd be there you said you'd help.
But all you do is hang out in the street.
For two weeks while I'm eight months, you leave.
No call, no visit, but you dawg me, I can't believe.
After all we been through, this is how it is.
No good-bye, no kind of sign, no hug, no kiss.
Why do you do this without a reason?
In my heart it's no longer the warm season.
It's like you put my heart in the dirt.
Now your back and I fall for you again.
Never did I think I'd come after your friend.

They come first, ha, and then came me.
I call soon our baby we'll see.
Everyday your son is in your arm.
I would've never thought you'd bring him harm.
Again you leave for another two weeks.
You said you work late baby, please.
I know you're outside with your friends on the street.
What happened to our future, our family?
I'll just ask the ones you left us for.
You just keep on driving my heart to the floor.
And I just watch out the window, I peak.
Where is the old you in which I seek?
I never thought in front of your son, you friends came too.
But I know one thing I have to leave you.
Me leaving after all the tries, lies and tears you brought.
Ha, I guess
You Never Would have thought...

Switch

The arguing, fighting, doing, saying what you don't mean.
How could it get to a point that I've never seen.
It's over, it's not, what do I do.
I don't even know how to act with you.
I know but I don't, I ask but I try to hold on.
I think but I don't know, what I should say, to go on.
You drive me crazy you say trust in you, please.
But you don't give me a reason for you are a tease.
You fill me up then let me drop down so low.
This roller coaster relationship, love life, affair.
How do I know that you really about me care?
It's seems so sweet as long as it's within your wish.
To say, to do, according to this.
I wonder why you decided to lock me in.
When your heart, love, and everything I'd never win.
It's always something every time I turn around.
It's like you apologize to see how fast I hit the ground.
So why? I wish I knew but I guess that's between God and you.
You are the only one I know that always got an excuse.
It's always someone else fault what's the use.
As much of a man as you are, you can never

man up.
I guess you just keep filling my holey cup.
I've been hurt; I've been played and abused.
But I not once tried to take it out on you.
Now that I look through the mirror and see.
I don't even recognize the reflection as me.
Who are you and where did I stray.
To ever become the one to act this way.
To listen and search for the unknown.
To top off the situation I've blown.
What happened to me after the words, I do.
I guess I lost track of the progress made and I turned into......YOU!

The Time has Come

I can't, no I won't, put up with this.
I don't know you, but the old you, I miss.
I know people change but not so severe.
One day we're happy, how did we get here.
I don't understand how you can say you love me.
When you get mad or whatever it be.
You leave me to fend for myself crying.
I can't, no I won't let my heart keep trying.
I've tried so many times and, so desperately.
But every time it always ends up me lonely.
I can't, no I won't keep pretending that everything's okay.
When what's hurting, you don't let me say.
Yeah, okay you ask what's wrong.
But I can see you getting mad cause it's taking too long.
No time for me in your schedule.
Run the streets with your friends, I'll let you.
Because now you don't have to worry about us.
You can't have a relationship without trust.
You left me for a week or so.
No calls, no visit THEN I should've let you go.
But no I just knew you would come back.
Yeah, you did but a lot of things you lack.
Like enough time for me, you don't even

ask how I'm doing.
Do I miss you of course, but me you're slowly away shooing?
How can over and over I love you, you say.
And with you your love walks away.
I can't cry no more I have to be strong.
My love for you was right but you did me wrong.
I can't no I won't stay here to see.
If with me is where your heart wants to be.
It's a little too late you should open your eyes.
Now you don't have to think of a lot of lies.
To cover why you didn't do what you said you would do.
Because now it's time to say I have to leave you.
Because your friends see you hear you laugh more than me.
And you're always asking "Why you tripping."
You don't need no extra time, stay with us.
'Cause for me to leave you the time has come.

One More Try!

It's always that one more chance, one more try.
You think things are good then you find out it's a lie.
The whispers in your ear of a better day.
And over night that whisper just fades away.
You slowly realize then exactly that the whisper is a cry.
"I know I'm wrong but baby please, if you give me one more try."
You know you shouldn't, it'll be just like last time.
Yet you keep trying to make lemonade with a lime.
People tell you that the best things in life are free.
But you soon realize that free, isn't all it's cracked up to be.
So what do you do when you're lost, confused but know what to do.
You call on the one who whispers in your ear," I Love You Boo!"
You cry on his shoulder I love you, why can't it work.
Then days later he's still that same jerk.
You know you love him dearly but y'all can't get along.
Over and over you do it, time and time

again.
Only to find out that now he has a new friend.
In the back of your mind, you are wondering how and why.
Although you know the answers of when and where, you just, cry.
Even though you can't take it no more.
You can Never seem to get your feet to walk out the door.
You love him so much, yet love is blind.
Since love don't see, there is no out of sight out of mind.
You don't believe over time your heart'll heal, you want it fixed right
then and there.
Then you call him again and he's right back where.
Into your life and in your heart.
Although you know y'all should be apart.
Only thing you hear is the whisper that's really a cry.
And for the sake of your heart you give it "One More Try."

Little Things

All the things I've been through, all the times I cried.
I guess love has never worked for me, how many times I've tried.
I've given it my all, I put everything to rest.
Yet, still this heart of mine is still in my chest.
I guess this love thing is one thing I'd always "almost have".
The good thing about it, after awhile, about it I'll just laugh.
At all the memories all the days.
His soft and loving laugh his charming, loving ways.
The way he use to smile at me with that seductive grin.
The way he use to look at me as though he could see within.
The way he use to touch me and I'll just melt like cheese.
Everything about him to me was just a tease.
I loved the way he watched me as I went to sleep.
As though he was an angel watching over me.
I never really understood why about him I cared.
I guess I'm not suppose to as long as it's

something we shared.
Like the bed we slept in every night.
Even our petty arguments and our occasional fight.
The love we shared for one another and my son.
I guess it's a lot of good to me he has done.
Maybe my heart is out of my chest.
Maybe he took it and laid it down to rest.
No longer did I have to worry about it, who would care.
Because my heart with me is not even here.
I guess it's too late for the knowledge I no longer lack.
Because now he has given me my heart back.

LOVE (As a Person)

When I first met you Love you was so sweet.
Your touch, your kiss would knock me off my feet.
I use to love the way we laughed, Love.
And the way you use to comfort me!
You were the one I ran to, when there was no other.
Now you have abandoned me Love for another.
How could you have done this Love, went astray?
You could not have picked anything other than today.
I don't know what I've done, but it's not my fault.
Love you was my teacher, you should have taught.
Told me what you wanted, Love so I would've knew.
But what you wanted is me not to be with you.
Love if God sent you here, why did you leave?
For us to be happy you have to believe that through all obstacles we will make it.
But Love we are out, after one time being hit.
So Love if you could tell me the reason

why.
And Love, I want to know, without a lie.
Love I thought we were meant to be.
But now I see Love you never loved me.

Like Father, Like Son

Oh Son, Oh Son!
You've treated my daughter the way I've done.
You do not appreciate her and you promise thing she'll never see.
Oh son, don't be the way I use to be.
Treat her with respect for she is a mother too.
And she will always love and trust you.
Never will she ever threaten to leave.
Because in you she can always believe.
But the more you do her wrong the more you will see.
She will lose all faith and love in you, like she's done me.
That is a bad feeling for you will never want in your heart.
Because it's then son, you and your love will be apart.
Treat her like you want someone to treat your mother and sister,
please do!
Because she is someone's' mother and sister too!
Why don't you see she has been through a lot of pain because of me.
It's your turn to try and be the man she knows you can be.
Or then you will see her out the door walk.

And then it will be too late for that talk.
You'll realize you really don't miss a good thing until it's gone.
You'll also see how hard it is to be alone.
Since you promised that change one to many times.
She won't be your girl, like she's not mine.
She found a man just like her father.
And everything I've done, he's done to her.
We've bruised her and robbed her loving heart.
Now over the years we have grown apart.
To lose the one you love, cherish, and respect.
Oh Son, don't you see.
Don't grow to be just like me.
Love her for she is a mother and sister too.
And then she will do all the things you need her to do.

My Lover, My friend

I love you, I do, but what's the use of that.
I should ask you do you love me, as a matter of fact.
How can I live feeling, what I tried so hard to prevent.
It seems like to me no one stays, my heart is for rent.
Can you feel this my lover, my friend.
Why do I hold on for the pain to come again?
I'm really tired of crying, I'm not going to do it anymore.
I'm really tired of trying love, so I closed my hearts' door.
You'll never understand that every day, I cry myself to sleep.
But over my life I wouldn't expect you to weep.
That's not what I want so don't get the idea from me.
Because my friend, I don't need your sympathy.
I've almost enclosed everything I want to say.
Now I understand with me it has to stay.
No one should know of the tears I've shed.
Because life is hard with all the pain I lead.
It grows but I can't give in to the sorrow.
Because my future is what I'll work on

tomorrow.
I guess I'll always be an easily hurt girl.
But what is life without pain in the world.
My pain will end and so will the rain.
No more crying for me no more pain.
I'm in a better place, I will reach the sky.
I loved you and missed you, all that is no lie.
Because my lover, I'll be leaving my friend.
I don't think that this time, I'll come back again.

Reasons

The way it use to be, the way it is now.
Makes me think if you ever loved me and how.
You treat me as if I'm nothing more than a friend.
It's hard but I have to say it's the end.
I rather be your friend cause you seem to treat them right.
Now you don't have to worry about arguing, we don't have to fight.
Whatever happened to, I love you with all my heart.
I guess your friends came and took that apart.
How could you just pick them over me?
How could you just leave me be?
Without an explanation, without a reason why.
I just wish sometimes that you didn't have to lie.
I mean, what is it that they do for you?
Why is it that no longer am I you're boo?
You don't even take care of your responsibility.
Well now you don't have to worry about that you see.
All I ever wanted from you was you.
Now that I realize it, you've changed that too.

The man I use to love is no longer around.
Now you're more like a street hound.
You rather be there, than here with me.
So now you, I will just let that be.
You have changed on me more than the seasons.
So I'm leaving for those reasons

Point of No return…..

Quiet Before the Storm

Nothing to look forward to you shattered my dreams.
Whatever I find, I'll think that it's not what it seems.
I'll look for the fault in whatever I cross.
I'm looking for something, but it got me lost.
I now know I stayed to long and I'm empty inside.
I will admit, you took me for a nice ride.
I thought you still loved me, I guess I was wrong.
I thought you was acting different, to be sure took too long.
It's funny our good outweighed our bad.
I guess its because when it got bad it made my heart sad.
I don't blame you though 'cause I blame me.
It got worse before it got better, but I couldn't see,
We yell, we scream, we would fight all day.
We were just saying things, we didn't mean to say.
I thought that we were better than this.
Those would be the memories, I would miss.
They say everyone wants sunshine, but hate the rain.
I guess this is something that the best of us go through.
But your rain, your rain made a drastic change in you.

Drunken Love

You go out, you splurge, you buy a drink or two.
You a grown up, you can do what you want to do.
But take a look around and tell me what you see.
More drinks, drunks, and singles, someone you don't want to be.
You go home, you stumble in, you slur hello to your sober lover & good friend
While they shake their head, thinking when will this all end.
Never once do you get it, that your love is running dry.
And sooner or later your love will be saying goodbye.
You talked about it over and over again, but nowhere it got.
Because you still come back talking about the latest bar is hot.
Your love wants time as your lover hopelessly tries to make it work.
But your friends call and now an unwanted fight lurk.
So now you can leave, because only she matters now, but she will only love
you for the moments due.
Because she doesn't love at all, she don't see you for you.
You're blinded by her strong hold and her mixed taste.

Now at home all the pieces are falling apart and you run to her for the paste.
But she can't help you, she can only make you forget.
The more you have her the more the pieces of your life don't fit.
Because you had everything but you traded it in for her and her crowd.
Now that she's gone, now that you're unwound.
Your life is not the same, it all slipped past without you ever to know.
She's never loved you now your lover had to go.
As you sit there with time to think.
Now all the arguments about "her" starts to really in you sink.
That the lover you had left because drinking was....
(In your lovers' eyes)
The one thing you couldn't let go, but most of all, the effects it had on
you made you naïve.
So the mention of letting it go made you angry and leave.
The last thing I needed was for you to look up with those drunken eyes
Then say all the painful things you can say to justify why.
The thought alone of the pain I can't bear.
And these thoughts to you I won't ever share.
You're at the spot with your drink by your side.
And I'm gone now so now "she" helps you again with another problem you hide.

Battered

Hitting, punching, kicking and screaming.
This is the work of a demon.
You love me, you hate me, you're sorry,
You're not.
These are the words that I've heard a lot.
I'm tired I've packed I'm leaving good-bye.
You say you're sorry, I know, I won't anymore with tears in your
eye.
I turn back around and slowly close the door.
Because again, you promise not to hurt me no more.
I know that you're lying, I know that you will.
But I come back to you, I forgive you still.
They say you could kill me.
They say next time it will be.
But I can't hear them their words fall on deaf ears.
Even though they only speak of my biggest fears.
I pray and I pray to the lord above.

Please God help me to find love.
What else am I to do, who am I to call.
When I try to leave it seems like the door is down a long hall.
Every step I take closer it moves a mile away.
I hate what you do, I want to leave, I love you, I stay.
I'm confused they say, follow your heart.
But my heart is what's tearing me apart.
I'm sick and tired but don't know what to do.
I need help now I need a hand to this get through.
I've lied and covered it up, to many times, I'm done.
Hitting, kicking, punching, and screaming.
That was the work of the demon.
That lives inside that lover of mine.
Now I can see it, no longer am I blind.
They said you could kill me.
But this time it won't, because I finally heard them, my ears are
clear.
And you hurting me is no longer a fear.

9 Months

Month 1

You found out your having me.
You and the outside world I can't wait to see.

Month 3

You've prayed and prayed to the lord above.
Now you finally have someone to love.

Month 4

You get the ultrasound you find out I'm a boy.
You're so happy you are crying tears of joy.

Month 5

Oh no, what's going on punching, kicking hitting me all in my head.
What's this my water is turning all red.

Month 7

He's back the one that made us bleed get away mommy.
He'll hurt us, he don't love you if he don't love me.

Month 9

I feel no push why don't you set me free.
The water that use to be here is no longer with me.
I feel the doctors pulling me from above.
Oh the joy it would be to feel love.
But I heard the doctors say that we've lost him too.
Oh mother please don't tell me I've lost you.

Day 3

In a merry place we meet again.
And my eternal life with you I spend.
I still hear you cry and your saying you're sorry.
Sadly knowing that because of you, the world I'll never see.

Call For Help

The truth of the matter is this:
He swung his hand and what I got was a fist
A rush to my body that took me down
Like I had the ball, is how I hit the ground.
Swinging my hands and kicking my feet
Screaming and yelling for him to get off me
He twisted my wrist, he'll break my arm
I started to search for anything to grab
To get him away, to get him off of me
I searched with my hand I never looked to see.

I swung it at the one causing me pain
I never knew it would be more of a lost than a gain.

Some point in the commotion he let me go
He spoke some words that I didn't know
He said he's hurt and started to bleed
Oh how I'm so sorry, that I didn't mean
I hurt my one, I can't believe I did that to he.

But I don't understand, how he could hurt me
Both bodies in pain now the baby begins to cry
My wrist bone pops and I can't understand why
I try to grab my baby, but it hurts so bad
Now again I break down, to not feed him makes me sad
Feeling low and depressed as that man of mine, talk
I ask for help and out again he begin to walk
I struggle and struggle to embrace the hurt, oh

the pain
I grab my baby and feed him as my eyes begin to rain.

Knock, knock, knock the police is at the door
What happened here tonight an accident to them doesn't matter anymore
They crowd around as to visualize the events of the night
But as I speak to them it doesn't come out right
I try and I try to explain, to make them see
Yes, he is hurt but he was hurting me
No one to care, so blind to my pain, mine is not for them to see
No regard for the pain inflicted upon me

Turn around you lie, you monster, you're under arrest
That's what they said, that's what they painted me as, they did it the best

No charges pressed, because we both was in the wrong that night
But the way it was wrote, I was wrong he was right
That's not the truth I never meant for him to bleed
To stop hurting, to be released, for him to get off, is what I need
I know "my sorry" won't make them understand or see
But I am a battered woman that they won't let free

Over and over, I played it in my mind, sorry and why, still races past
Now I can't eat or sleep I don't know how long I will last
I been depressed, I been asking for help, for someone to talk
My children out my life just snatched away, they didn't walk
Now it builds up all over again
I'm asking for help, but I'm enclosed no one to help my broken mind mend
So I say to you hello is anyone there, for me
I don't know how much longer, how strong I can be
Goodbye is what will be my final words to say
Cause no one cares or understands, I didn't mean to, I can't live this way

Writing use to be my only escape, my only way out
But to leave for good, writing helping I surely doubt
Its only two ways out of this mess
They hear and understand my cry for help or
_____ you know the rest
   Good-bye

Guilty as Charged

I understand you want to walk away
I understand there's nothing left to say

How could "I" love you and treat you that bad?
How could "I" love you and make you so sad?

But before we part and you put your things by the door
Let me say something, please let me have the floor.

"Where were you, when I needed a hug
What was your role in separation when life gave our love a test

What did you hear when I needed to talk
What tear did you catch, when my eyes they began to stalk

How was your absence, any better than my words
How was your lacking, any better than the way I receive.
I had goals too, but where were you to believe

How about all the pain in my heart that you can't understand

Or when I was single and alone, but you were my man

How is it that everything else came before little ole me
Yet, my constant attempts to get time, nagging is all you see

Please, explain to me how your love for me suddenly came to a hault
but none the less my love, "this is all my fault"

I see the mistakes I made, the evidence is very clear to see
I demanded and pushed away, while you didn't understand and neglected me
The only difference between the two, is not whose wrong, whose right
It's that you deny your part in the dark, and I regret mines in the light

Can't you see what I needed that came out in the form of demand
All I asked for was time, love, attention and the heart of my man
If that's a crime, I'm guilty as charged, please charge me
But don't overlook your charges, because you're as guilty as me!

2 Sided

Why does it seem so hard to see, that I am hurting too
(or) that I can endure heartache and pain just like you
I've been used and abuse ran down and hurt
I've had my heart pulled out and stomped in the dirt
Are you blind to my torture, because I'm suppose to stand tall
Or do you mock me as if i have no feelings at all
What about my burden, my sorrows and regret
What about the love and affection I didn't get
What about the constant betrayal and deceit
Or how about the unfaithfulness that knocked me off my feet
or maybe it was the tears I stayed up to cry
The "why me's", the "I thought you loved me", but you lie
The constant arguements just to leave and stay out cause you can
But I guess it doesn't matter, because I'm a man

I can't let go of the past hurt and pain
I also stayed up at night as my eyes began to rain
I wished on a star that this could work and you'd stay
I prayed to God over and over again
I had no one to consult, couldn't run to family or

friend
To show that I was broken, my pride I just couldn't bend
Oh how I yearned that one day it would change
Yet, every time I thought it did, you'd move further out of range
To love again is not something I'll try to give or get
Since the pain love caused me, I will always feel and regret

It hurts me deeply to know I've been battered inside
But I have to suck it up, be a man and my feeling I hide
I look at the world and say I'm ok, about my feelings, I lied
Because to admit it, out loud, is like a shot at my pride.

CYCLE(S)

I was a child you was suppose to protect me
I was helpless how could you not see
The fear in my eyes the hatred in my heart
The scar left behind as my skin was ripped apart
I cry now when you leave but only to be left behind
You look at me and still don't see, as you say,
"Please don't whine"
You let him you could've, should've stopped him the 1st time
Now I live my life wondering why you didn't pick up and leave
I pray to you, oh lord, to hold me tight as I walk this trail
As I release all this pain & memories that made my life a living hell
Oh lord, I pray to you above to make my pain another's lesson learned
Show the world, oh lord, how things done in the dark needs to come to light & be burned

In the basement, in my room on the floor balled up crying out
Battered and abused, screamed I tried, you saving me soon became a doubt
But how could you, you need help too
I pretend I'm asleep as I hear the thunder of pain come through
My walls, the floor, the screams through the door
I am a child forced to grow up to fast
How to protect you is the thought through my mind it past
I ran out screaming, "get off my mommy"
But he's too strong with hate in his eyes, he didn't see me

He felt threatened but by who, little ole me
How could he love you and how could you believe
Mommy please don't stay, we all need to leave
Another day you leave as you pretend not to see in my eye
The tears form and the fear of now it's my brothers and me, oh why
The kicking the punching as he say "oh you think you tough"
"Well after I'm done, you will be a little rough"
I say please I can't, I won't let you do this to them, please take I
"As he leaves he turns to say be careful what you ask, because you don't know what you'll get at the end"
You finally come home but only to see that we bleed, we hurt as much as you
Now you understand, we need you to get it together for us too
We finally one night sneak out of our house to grandmas
That was 15 years ago today, as I just woke to find at home, I'm back
My lady put me out for hurting, hitting, yelling at her
I guess he was right he would make it rough
For me to forget maybe we stayed to long now I became he
Trying to release my anger and control on to another, I would
Never hurt a child, but she I have no mercy, but I should
She is and you once were the same
She put me out her life, but do you see, you stayed now my scars are my shame.

Mistakenly Done

My heart is so heavy, I want to go (home)
Who?
What?
When
Where?
Why am I here?
I ask this question in a rhetorical sense
But I mean it to be answered
Although, I'm almost sure I know
Mistakes happen daily but none worth this
To be isolated and trapped with
No one to reach out to
Again I feel like my backs against a wall
I'm surrounded by people but
I have no one at all
I'm here but I'm not
If you know what that mean
No one was listening when I tried to come clean
I told all of the event as they unfolded that night
But they twisted my words
And now it's not right
Now I'm here and I want to go back
But yet again help for me, is something I lack.

Should've, Could've, would've

I said I would leave, but I didn't walk out the door
I said it wasn't worth it, yet and still I stayed
through all the tears, I believed in God
So I kneeled down and prayed in and out, ups and down are the norm
Love, relationship, tears, pain, good and bad it's all the same
Now it's took a turn and there's no turning back
Oh, how I wish I wouldn't have gotten off track
I sit here and I think about all that could've been
I think about where I would be if out the door I walked
Every day I cried for help with no one to talk
If only I wrote a letter, but I did for no one to read
If only I would have followed, with no one to lead
I couldn't see the future, I wish I could've, so I would know
What would happen, what mistakes would be made, if I didn't go
I should have fought harder, I should've lived in make-believe
What if I pretented so long, that it didn't hurt me
I could've made excuses or did that I succeed
It would've gotten better but that's not what I need
I should've seen it coming, I should've seen the change
Should've, could've, would've, yet and still I take the blame!

The Unseen Scars (of a battered woman)

No bruises to see, no wounds to heal
No words to describe the way I feel
How could you bless me and curse me with the same lips
How could you hold me and be the reason that my heart rips?
I prayed and prayed day in and day out
It got better, I thought, but then again I doubt
I ask myself over and over, how did I get here....

Then God answered;

"I have a lesson for you to learn is why you're here
I snatched you out of a situation as you needed me to do
I gave you answers, you ignored because you didn't want them to be true
Over and over I had to watch, you cry
As you heard and saw what you wanted and continued to try
Why my child did you not listen to me?
Why do I have to take all from you, just for you to see?
I love you so much and would never cause that kind of pain
I might test you my child, but because of me your eyes never saw rain
I sat you by yourself so you could have time to

reflect
The road you were taking had to be put in check
My child you know I never left you before
But I had to do something to make you walk out the door."

Oh, as I listen to the words that my father has said
I started to realize more, the scars was all in my head
They are not easily seen, but are harder to heal
Just because you don't see them, don't mean they're not real.

Double Victim

You can play crazy all you want, you see
But the truth will come out the truth will set you free
No one can ever know what I went through I feel no one will ever know, my
Hell on earth was real to argue, to fight, to try another day
Nothing can make me accept, why it didn't go that way
What could have been said, what value do things hold
That makes you put your hands on me, hurt me or be so cold
What words were a trigger, that put our love to death
The situations at night could've been either one of our last breath
The story that's real and the one that you're telling me
Oh if only someone would stop and really look, only then could they see
The tears, the pain, the fear that I held in my eye
To know that you promised to never hurt me, now you asking why
How you try to escape the facts that you struck first
And how you want to say that you dodged the hurst
Our bond under God, the secrets that hide
All the things I knew about, but yet you lied

The emotional build up, I held but failed to release
You couldn't handle the pressure of the world around
I guess that's why you came home to tear me down
But no more, no way can I do this again
Lack of communication, trust, love, and boundaries you failed to be my friend
I knew you at one point or so I thought
Yet, that lack of knowledge, oh what pain it brought
Running to tell, what people can't see, keeping the secret of what you did to me
I've been hurt and abused, you was suppose to keep me safe
But at the end it was more to it and now your one up
I guess you win the score is on your side
But just like you, my scars I can't hide
Every day I have to remember from the unseen scars you left
I asked, I begged, I cried out the words came out but your ears were dead
The way you hurt me left no visible mark
Here is your round of applause I guess that's another system you'll out smart
Here, the fact is I didn't paint the picture clear
No matter what someone says, picks up, holds that belongs to you
 It gives you no right to hurt them or try to teach them your way
A thought to all, please hear my pain through what

I say
One to many times, have I seen my death, through the eyes of a lover, a husband, a friend
To not know and see that in the blink of an eye, it could be you or he
That for life someone will fend
You know in your life when
The question, that change the situation has come don't stay it's too late, there's no recovery from there
I miss my life, my kids, the way it was before
Before all the chaos came breaking down my door but understand, I wish, I would have seen the coming, of
Destruction, pain and lies
I wish I could have known that right before my eyes
My whole world would change and it would go down hill
No one told me the voice to leave was real
I say to you today, leave before the irreversible come
Don't stay in a place and become a double victim

Domestic violence doesn't start physically it ends there. If you or anyone you know is in a destructive relationship, I know it's easier said than done, but you have to leave call for help don't be ashamed.

Overflow

*My babies, my children how could I not see
that the one I was loving , was not loving, we
There still are no words left to say to you
all I keep thinking to myself, is how I'm not
there with you
I'm weak, I hurt, I cry all day and night
I don't know where to start to make it alright
I left you because of a mistake, a mistake it
was
Why didn't I notice sooner, all that comes back
is, because
I'm so sorry, I apologize from somewhere deep
within
My cries for help is worthless, when it's you
who couldn't fend,
Off the attacks that were coming, for you
after I was gone, oh what am I to do
I can't hold you, protect you or speak on your
behalf
Because now I'm, to them, a monster to speak
now will make them laugh
Oh how the joke would be to me nothing but
pain
Oh how the thought of losing you forever drives
me insane
I prayed and I prayed for the cards to play out
when they land
Oh how I wish and I'm sorry to ever have loved*

that man
Words and actions from him I was never to expect
Toward someone so helpless he turned his back to neglect
I never meant for the tears to flow over to you
I shed enough that my sky turned gray from blue
Now it is storming the worst in my life
Boarded up my heart to protect what is left, behind
To protect myself, I didn't see, I crossed the line
Please forgive me for a choice, you didn't choose
Because my babies, my children, you I can't lose.

Lesson Learned

*As I sit here in a shell
Left with my thoughts
I wonder what the hell
After coming this far
I'm up, I fall
I have, they took
I'm left here abandoned
With my thoughts, let's take a look;*

"I don't remember exactly where
my life took it's turn
But oh how many times do you bump your head,
Until you learn
I've loved, I've lost, I had it all
Or so I thought
What is the value of those material things
A house, a car, jewelry, clothing and such
Why do we pay for them and value them so much
I never knew what was worthless,
priceless, invaluable to me
until one day I awake and no longer could I see
until one day I couldn't reach out and touch, feel, hear or see
something that I loved, cherished, and held

so dear
something I couldn't image a life lived without
something of the most value,
but priceless without a doubt
how could I be here in a shell left alone with my thoughts
how could I not consider, the effect of, the ripple to this something it would've brought
the smallest little thing in my messed up pond of life, love and pain
would grow to be a giant and nothing I would gain
how could I not make a better choice, for that, that does not chose
how could I not see the ripple if that something I was to lose
now that I'm left alone with my thoughts and that's all
I sit and I feel as my life begins to break down and fall
what could my angels, my children , my babies have done for my absence the earned
nothing at all, they never saw it coming because it's my,

lesson learned!

Us

Why does true love no longer exist?
Why when you love someone unconditional, it's this.
If you don't, if you won't, only because, just don't be you.
It can only work if you're who I want, too.
When I met you, you were so kind and caring and fun.
Now as we got closer it seems as from each others' embrace we run.
It takes two to love and it takes two to fall apart.
Sometimes I wonder though where will we end up.
As we walk around with feelings over flowing our cup.
People continue to ask me "what did you see in him."
Now I know you were the replacement of a missing limb.
We are so much the same yet so different in light.
I won't say it, yet you say it's too early to be right.
You can't believe, no you won't, in true love.
You don't think that happiness is a sign from above.

I care about you maybe more than you know.
And with fear of being the only one that's more than I'll show.
I don't know what to say, I don't know what to do.
It seems like you pushed so hard for me not to be with you.
We don't talk, communication for us is when an argument arise.
No longer do I hold you or look in your eyes.
You don't even notice the smile every time I see you.
Even if you just left and came back, that's just what you do.
I miss you when you're gone, yet for happiness want you to leave.
I sit and think to myself what will it take for you to believe.
I'm not asking for much, just a little more than I got.
If I was to tell you how I feel, to know my heart won't get shot.
As I sit I smile realizing that won't happen my heart's in a shell.
And it will stay that way because you I'll never tell.
And your heart is cold never to defrost.
So this is only a thought of mines, one that will soon be lost.

If there was a thing called love and it was still true.
I hope that its reality comes to you.

End of The Line

We make it our duty to give them what they need.
But in reality they're overwhelmed by greed.
A promise made, a promise never kept.
With that promise off your feet he swept.
They take our love and the sparkle in our eyes.
But in return they give us pain in which we disguise.
He'll never understand how rich and pure your heart seem.
You'll never know either, because for his love is what you dream.
We give all our thanks to God that we've found the one that's right.
But all we ever do is argue, fuss and fight.
At the end of the day we lay and close our eyes.
Not noticing what we need to realize.
He's still not here and we have started to cry.
Not once did he even notice not once did he say good-bye.
Is it that he's scared and his heart is also pure?
How do you know, how does anyone know for sure.
If he don't realize how much he needs you.
Then you shouldn't realize that you need him too!
Through the fire he takes you for you to get burned.
After all the lies, no good-byes and the tears in your eyes you, haven't learned.

*You did all possible that you can.
He doesn't know how to love a true woman.
He comes back with sweet words for you.
He never say sorry, he knows he was wrong, he just fill your heart
with "I love you too!"
but who was there for you when you cried late at night.
Where did you run, when y'all had a fight?
As you get up to start the fire in your heart again.
Your eyes will never tell you his heart you'll never win.
All you do is one day look at him and say so nice.
I ain't gonna be that same fool twice.
He'll then realize what a good woman he had lost, for good.
Because now you have done what you always could.
Left him to think and wonder why.
You just walked out and didn't say good-bye.
If you have to do everything his way.
For you and him, no honey let him go astray.*

DONE

*Time and time again, I got the short end.
Walk over you everyone else do, but I kissed your behind.
I let you do as you please, yell at me is all you do.
Turn around and love me now I'm your boo.
Use me until I'm dry as a bone,
I know now the love is gone.
You don't respect me you don't even care.
So why do you constantly come back here.
Because I'm the only one who cared and let you be.
But the benefit of the doubt you won't give to me.
I put you out in anger, you come back with rage.
You should know what's good and what's bull at your age.
I guess not, under the influence or another we constantly fight.
To be here for you it takes all my might.
What am I to do now that I'm fed up with you?
Because you don't want to stay but what they say is true.
You turned your back on me, but expect me to be here for you.
Never again, let the ones who care enough to talk be there for you.*

Reconstruction….

I Use To (Intro)

I use to love but now I don't.

To love again, no, I can't, I won't.

I frown now, I use to smile.

But for love my heart has traveled awhile.

Why can't the love, the smile come back to me?

What do I do to be and stay happy...!

After the storm

After the scars heal(ed) and you slowly drift apart
Everything is in shambles, you try to make sense of your heart
"Ups" and "downs" you're use to, but this is too much
How and why, mixed emotions, of such
Who hurt who and all the pain that's left
How could we have done and said such things, to someone we love
I still love you, but I can't take it anymore
But, if you say it will work, I won't walk out the door
Deep down I know this is not what I need
But it's what I have and it's all for me
Why can't I see, how am I so confused
Why don't I realize, I've been used and abused
Why can't I stand, to walk away from this fantasy
When I know it can't work and the hurt you caused you'll never see

What would it be like to truly let go and move on
Will I truly heal from the unseen scars
Or will I torture myself by continuosly picking the scab
And everyone I meet will have to pay for the last
As soon as "it" triggers the thought of things from my past
I will bring to the table my pain and make them pay
Then the storms come again and together we can't stay

How do you let go of pain from the scars unseen
How do you give someone else a slate to start that's clean
Why do they have to pay for the past one's mistakes
Because the pain I can't see, but I feel, isn't truly gone away
I could only guess that we give ourselves time and space to heal
And don't lie to ourselves and say that you let go and it's not real
We all have been hurt, but we don't give ourselves time
Maybe, that's why the same pain keeps reoccurring(hurting) in our lives

The rebound is a lie you can't truly get over one loves hurt and pain by getting replacing it with another. Allow yourself time to reboot and figure out what you will and will not take next time. Make sure you truly are ready and have closure, forgiveness is the key.

Love ?

What is love?
Oh, but something I deeply yearn for
through all the clouds and trials
I know it's worth having
all to myself, yet enough to share with all
The ups and downs, just to get it right
The rushing sensation when you find peace
after the fight
The unconditional, forgiveness, tender gentle
touch
Of someone who vow to never let it get past a
few exchanged words
Love as it seems, is a very invisible, sight to see
That comes with all the dressings of, does love,
love me?
How could you have possibly doubted a more
sweeter thing
A more sweeter touch, kiss, embrace that's so
real
Despite what you see, love is what you feel!

Questions

How could you not see all the love I have for you?
How could you constantly ignore the (things) wrong you do to me that hurt so bad
So what, I wanted all your time
So what, I wanted attention from you, I couldn't, why?
I loved you deeply, so pure, I supported your dream
But what you needed and wanted, is not as simple as it seem
How can you get what you need, if you don't know what you need
How can you have the good, if all you give is bad
How can you not notice my love is pure, and make me sad?
How dare you deny my request to be treated like the Queen you called me?

How dare you say "you know my worth", and still put the world before me?
I still cry from the pain, bruises and the scars, you left.
I still want what I had, even though, it's not worth it

I loved you so much I put you in front of, me
I still don't understand why, my love for you, you couldn't see
Why didn't you appreciate all I had to give
Why be so selfish with something so simple, so free
Why take all the mistakes of your past loves, out on me
I gave and gave and gave all you did was receive
I knew it was on the rocks yet, I still didn't leave
I tried to wait it out, as if love comes in a wave
You said, I led and showed you to my heart, a way I paved
But you took a detour and left me, alone
Now I sit here full of what I gave and you are, gone
I guess I can say goodbye to all I thought to be
Because the truth is you never loved me.

The Line is So Thin

How quick the line can be crossed to the other side
You loose track of what it meant, you to be, rebound, no you lied
To think or believe we'll be back after all that's been done
In my arms for love and support you can never again run
I forgive you, I'll get through, but I'll never forget who you turned into
The one I despise, the one I no longer know
I looked in your eyes, to your heart, but where did it go
We argue, we fight, we make up, it's alright
Our days was long, but we slept at night
How could you allow it to slip past, our point of no return
How could it get here then the bridge gets burned
I love you's become a thing of the past
Oh, I cry and hope for change how long can we last
Ups and downs are expected to come, but now its to far

Rewind let's take it back a notch, where did it begin, where is credit due

Fast forward how you point the finger like it wasn't you too
Play, to continue on and soon it will end
Pause is what you need to at least salvage me as a friend
The remote is broken or is it that it's real life
Not too long before we were friends until, I am your wife
One signature and a phone call later, we're at it again
But now the war has begun and no thought left to be a friend
How could the line be there for no one to see
To cross at will, for us to go too far off, never to return to me.

Woman Scorned

I see you, for who you are trying to hide
In your heart that show through your eyes
Instead of fessing up to your part, you sit in a cocoon
Singing the why's
I tried to look past, I tried to accept, I even tried to help
You made it clear, you made me regret you even pushed me away
Now you're including, what's left, saying I should just stay
Don't hold my love, my passion, my heart to control
Let go and look in the mirror because you're fighting the soul

I no longer am equipt, with the power of love and healing through words
Because when I tried, you attacked, my heart poured out, haven't you heard
It was drowned, stabbed, buried and left for dead
And when I thought no more could come, you attacked my head
Now you unblocked what I hid, because of the power no one should have
There's no hell like a woman scorned and she

gets the last laugh
Why, how could you, I thought, but nooo you started with me, ended with you
I loved you, you pretended, I was there to support, you broke down
Now go join the circus they need you, clown
Jokes on whoever thought the game was in a man's hometown
I may have come from a rib located in the chest
But God worked extra hard on me and at this I'm the best
I gave birth to man many times after your one life given to me
I gave you the most precious part of me, my reason and my way
You took my vows and through them, you shredded each and everyday

I'm not to be bitter, or sad, or cry after the game is done
I plan on shaking hands with the opponent, it was forced, yet fun
To watch how skills are a gift and sharpened upon use
To see your face when together, the power moves, we could have made you chose to abuse
Can we please bounce back before we hit the point of no return
Before I begin a lesson that you will regret to

learn
All I want is to at least exist in a world, even if seperated from you
That I won't have to build, protect and then plot and plan too
It is a lot but none the less for mines i will do
Think about your next move for this is a call for truce and warning to you

A Tale of Two Hearts.....

A tale of two hearts that couldn't be, they loved each other deeply
Over and over they pushed each other away, but that they didn't see
But with all the pushing neither went astray, their love was Strong nothing could tear them apart.
Because their love was very strong from the start.
Out of that love came a miracle, a gift.
In away
That was the way to give them a lift.
All they need now is to open up and see.
That to love one another is to let the love be, being the stubborn people they were they broke each others heart.
Now they are thinking about their past as they live apart.
 The moral of this tale is that love is strong, don't be that one to find out what you had when that one is ... Gone!

Good-Bye Past

You filled me up with this tender thought.
I could have never seen the pain it brought.
The signs were obvious, but still them I ignore.
I have to leave you, but instead I want you more.
Instead of being the real me, that I hide.
I heard you say I love you and you lied.
If you cared you wouldn't have hurt me.
What happened to us or the love that use to be?
I knew what it was I wrote that book.
But when the clues are in your face, you don't look.
You made your way into my heart.
So you could from the inside rip it apart.
We use to laugh and joke around.
What we had, happiness, I thought I found.
What is it about love stories that always go bad?
Why do most of them have the woman so sad?
Tell me one thing before I go.
What was the problem, I need to know?
What was it that lead us apart?
Could it have been the gentleness of her heart?
Or was it the way she kissed you on your lips.
Well guess what, that feeling come and go take the tips.

She'll never do the things, I did for you.
She could never listen to you the way I do.
Hey if that's what you want, you get what you deserve.
I'll just watch you from the curb.
Because when she hurt you, the way you've done me.
You'll know that every change have a cost, but love is free.
You filled me up and let me go.
What was the problem I need to know?
You rarely called; you're never able to talk.
Either you're at the store or down the walk.
What is it that they did for you?
I didn't want to give it up, we could've talked it through.
But I guess it's too late no longer can it last.
The best part of us is now the past.
A real man could've got out before he got to deep.
I guess the road you took was too steep.
I don't know how this problem even came.
Prayer that you would change, the signs that it's the same.
My mind told me this love, I shouldn't keep.
For my heart to stay this long the love was deep.
I have a good and strong heart, I'll make it through.

I need a man who'll understand that, not you
You don't know what your heart is for, as you've shown.
One minute you're feeling it, then the feelings are gone.
I must admit you got me at the end.
Your heart I thought I would win.
You did fill me up with a tender thought.
This pain, I never suspected, it would've brought.
The signs were clear, but them I did ignore.
I should've left, but I wanted you more.
I don't understand was it Temptation or Fate?
It could've been a Change of Heart you recognized too late.
All I know is that it's over for sho'.
Now excuse me my love I have to go!!

Love Yourself

No one will understand when all has gone wrong.
No one can say that you have to be strong.
Only you know the pain you feel inside your heart.
Only you can take the pain that ripped you apart.
So when you're at your worst and feel blue.
Look to the mirror and say "I love you".
If that's not enough go out for some air.
When you come back from clearing yourself, the pains not there.
See how good it feel to go and take time for you.
While you're at it take time to find you too.
Once you love yourself whatever your situation, maybe.
You'll get through it with your head high you'll see.
If you don't remember anything remember this:
"Once you love and find yourself the past you won't miss".

If you can't look to yourself first, don't look to another.
Find yourself because you are your first lover.
Do for you and God will do for you too! Because, help comes to those who help themselves.

LOVE YOURSELF...

If you won't no one else will.

Suicide

After a long deep thought, after heavy consideration
I came to the conclusion; I have to change, led by determination

I switched back and forth from the pros and cons
I'm not sure if it's worth all the effort or the deep thought,
But it has to be done, a conclusion has to be sought
Do I chose a day, time, place, do I write a letter, to paint a picture of goodbye
There's no time for me to accept or flood out, why
I just know that the old me has to die

To give way for the new me that can't wait to be born
To show off the things I've learned, that can't wait to be free
All of the old things that use to be done
I have to kill them quickly; they're no longer, me

I am renewed, reborn, made over a new person that's finally complete
The transformation I had to overcome and complete, had completely broke my pride
It broke me inside and out, left me with no

other choice but, suicide
I was left with my thoughts, when there was nothing to think
The consequences of those old actions, as quickly in me, began to sink
So I pulled back my tears and faced my old ways
I told my reflection that I am counting down the days
And soon enough there will only be me
Suicide, of my old ways is the only way to set me, free

In order to become reborn you have to "kill" the old YOU. Learn from your mistakes
and become a new way.

A Broken Heart is Never Broken

I sit here and think why we endure the thought
Of letting someone in and soon pain it brought
I let you all the way in, I never will again
I handed it all over, now I don't even have a friend
I loved you and honored you from deep down inside
You ran, you bought, your not here, you lied
You led me astray with the strings on my hand
You used and abused took me for granted and ran
How could I let you tear me away from my heart?
Hold it in your hand and watch you shred it apart
Little by little slowly with pain in my eyes
You did the unthinkable and left me full of whys
No one will get there again, when they ask me why
I'll say because my heart can't mend
Broken in despair with a gut full of grief and regret
My heart is building a force field and my mind is set
I will walk away and leave as you've asked me to do
But I know, that I will always love you
I love you enough to let go and let you be happy without me
Just know that I'm leaving as well to be where I

can be
Appreciated, understood, loved, partnered with trust and loyalty
I also deserve someone who will love me for me

Goodbye I say as I see you as mine for the last time
Goodbye to you love as you conquer new chapters in life
Thank you and I appreciate you making me your wife
I never meant to hurt you or make you feel regret
As for me this is not as good as it get.

Thanked and Forgiven

Thank you to the one who taught me, the best lesson of all
It's about the words you said to me and how I know you lie
It's about the attempt to break me and my individual thought
But look a little closer at the pain you brought
It's about the bruise you didn't leave around my eye
You taught me the true meaning of "Love shouldn't hurt"
That when someone truly love you, they wouldn't verbally attack your heart
You wouldn't take for granted the love that I held so true to me
You would've appreciated and protected my love and concerns, that's how it should be
You taught me that there is no specific place
When you're in love, to the top, there's no race
I would like to unofficially thank you for the lesson I went through
I paid off the debt of the ones who did it to you
I forgive you for all the comfort, love and words not said
I forgive you for not letting it all go; the comparison was all in your head
I forgive you for the attempted murder of my heart
I forgive you for it all and leave it all behind, as a new I start.

Reconstruction (complete)

What to expect in the days to come
What emotions to make of where I came from
How close in days, I wait to see
The way of my new life, who I've grown to be
Up's and downs, all around, a beautiful change
The old me is dead and gone killed by close range
One change in the ripple, that use to be habit
Took me awhile to gather and collect the strength, but now I got it
Got to put myself first and don't take from the forward move
To lead a new life I had to set up a new rule
Don't be fooled it takes more time for what it's worth
I can't, but I wouldn't change any parts of my birth
The life that I'm destined to live forever and now
Will pay me in amounts of lessons learned and growth
The things that's offered, the struggle that came
As silly as it sounds it was worth all the hurt and pain
Sometimes I wished for a different path, led
All that comes to mind is "It could've been worst", as said
I know that I'm stronger, better and wiser the least
When my pieces reformed and the sculpture is

formed
All that I see now is a second chance
conceived
All from the struggle and the deepest love
believed
That came from my journey I traveled above all
I made it through the storm and now I stand,
tall.

The New Beginning……

CPSIA information can be obtained
at www.ICGtesting.com
Printed in the USA
FFOW04n1951110516
23987FF

9 781943 274307